INTO Wild California

BLACKBIRCH®
PRESS

THOMSON
GALE

San Diego • Detroit • New York • San Francisco • Cleveland • New Haven, Conn. • Waterville, Maine • London • Munich

THOMSON

GALE

© 2004 by Blackbirch Press™. Blackbirch Press™ is an imprint of The Gale Group, Inc., a division of Thomson Learning, Inc.

Blackbirch Press™ and Thomson Learning™ are trademarks used herein under license.

For more information, contact
The Gale Group, Inc.
27500 Drake Rd.
Farmington Hills, MI 48331-3535
Or you can visit our Internet site at http://www.gale.com

LIBRARY OF CONGRESS CATALOGING-IN-PUBLICATION DATA

Into wild California / Elaine Pascoe, book editor.
    p. cm. — (The Jeff Corwin experience series)
Based on an episode from a Discovery Channel program hosted by Jeff Corwin.
Summary: Television personality Jeff Corwin takes the reader on an expedition through California, and introduces some of the diverse wildife found there.
Includes bibliographical references and index.
    ISBN 1-56711-858-5 (alk. paper) — ISBN 1-4103-0178-8 (pbk. : alk. paper)
    1. California—Description and travel—Juvenile literature. 2. Natural history—California—Juvenile literature. 3. Corwin, Jeff—Journeys—California—Juvenile literature. [1. Zoology—California. 2. California—Description and travel. 3. Corwin, Jeff.] I. Pascoe, Elaine. II. Corwin, Jeff. III. Discovery Channel (Firm) IV. Series: Jeff Corwin experience

F866.2.I67 2004
591.9794—dc21   2003007523

Printed in China
10 9 8 7 6 5 4 3 2 1

E ver since I was a kid, I dreamed about traveling around the world, visiting exotic places, and seeing all kinds of incredible animals. And now, guess what? That's exactly what I get to do!

Yes, I am incredibly lucky. But, you don't have to have your own television show on Animal Planet to go off and explore the natural world around you. I mean, I travel to Madagascar and the Amazon and all kinds of really cool places—but I don't need to go that far to see amazing wildlife up close. In fact, I can find thousands of incredible critters right here, in my own backyard—or in my neighbor's yard (he does get kind of upset when he finds me crawling around in the bushes, though). The point is, no matter where you are, there's fantastic stuff to see in nature. All you have to do is look.

I love snakes, for example. Now, I've come face to face with the world's most venomous vipers—some of the biggest, some of the strongest, and some of the rarest. But I've also found an amazing variety of snakes just traveling around my home state of Massachusetts. And I've taken trips to preserves, and state parks, and national parks—and in each place I've enjoyed unique and exciting plants and animals. So, if I can do it, you can do it, too (except for the hunting venomous snakes part!). So, plan a nature hike with some friends. Organize some projects with your science teacher at school. Ask mom and dad to put a state or a national park on the list of things to do on your next family vacation. Build a bird house. Whatever. But get out there.

As you read through these pages and look at the photos, you'll probably see how jazzed I get when I come face to face with beautiful animals. That's good. I want you to feel that excitement. And I want you to remember that—even if you don't have your own TV show—you can still experience the awesome beauty of nature almost anywhere you go—any day of the week. I only hope that I can help bring that awesome power and beauty a little closer to you. Enjoy!

Best Wishes!
Jeff

INTO
Wild California

They call it the Golden State, and for me it's a gold mine. We're going to travel from the ocean to the mountains, from the city to the desert, and find out how the animals in California manage to survive with all the people that live here.

I'm Jeff Corwin.
Welcome to California.

San
Francisco

Santa
Cruz

Monterey
Bay

California's rugged coast is breathtaking!

Say hi to my friend Sean.

Our adventure begins off the coast of Santa Cruz, where I'm going to introduce you to the apex predator— the top ocean predator—of these California waters. We're going to do a little fishing with Sean Van Sommeran of the Pelagic Shark Research Foundation, aboard his boat, a 21-foot Cris-Craft. Sean spends day after day out here waiting for the chance to see—and then tag—a great white shark. It's all part of a study to track both the movement and numbers of these extraordinary fish.

This is a major lure.

A bag filled with seal fat helps to lure.

Check out this lure—look at the size of it. It's actually in the shape of an adult female elephant seal. We're going to deploy this lure, wait for a great white shark to come up, and tag it. Besides the lure, we have a burlap bag filled with the tallow, or fat, of elephant seals, which are a primary food source for the sharks. No seals were harmed to get the tallow—it was harvested from a dead animal that had washed up on the beach. The tallow increases the probability that in this great ocean of water, we'll bring in that creature we've come to study. If we do, Sean's boat is equipped with an underwater camera so we can meet it eye to eye.

And we have a shark! He's just come up close to the lure. It's a great white shark—a shark that's capable of reaching lengths of 21 feet and more. This one's probably a 10 or 12 footer—not huge as great whites go, but plenty big for me. Holy cow! I've played with cheetahs and black mambas. I've danced with Asian bears, but I've never seen a great white shark alive. Look at his dorsal fin coming out of the water! Is that not cool? Do you see that gray dorsal surface? And that white belly? His eyes look like doll's eyes.

Look at that dorsal fin. Cool!

This guy's about 12 feet long.

He's got doll's eyes but he's no doll.

Look at those razors in his mouth.

Unfortunately, people have given the great white the reputation of being a monster. This shark is an eating machine, but it's more than that. Sharks are complex animals that have evolved over millions of years. They're *chondrichthyes*, cartilaginous fish, with an ancient ancestry. Understanding the fossil history of these animals is a challenge because their skeletons, made of cartilage, don't form fossils well. But we do

LOOK AT THIS!

The great white shark is probably the most feared fish in the ocean. These creatures are not any meaner than any other fish—it's just their reputation as top predators that have given them a bad name.

Great whites are one of the largest hunters in the ocean—they average 12–16 feet (3.7–4.9 m) long. The biggest great white shark ever recorded was 23 feet (7 m) long, and weighed about 7,000 pounds (3,200 kg). As with most sharks, females are larger than males. Shark pups can be over 5 feet (1.5 m) long at birth.

With an average of about three thousand teeth, a great white is a ferocious predator. Young great whites eat fish, rays, and other sharks. Adults eat larger prey, including pinnipeds (sea lions and seals), small toothed whales (like belugas), otters, and sea turtles. They also eat carrion (dead animals that they have found floating dead in the water). Great whites do not chew their food. Their teeth rip prey into mouth-sized pieces that are swallowed whole.

A big meal can satisfy a great white for up to two months.

Sharks primarily use their sense of smell, which is incredibly sensitive. A great white's nostrils can smell one drop of blood in 25 gallons (100 L) of water.

These amazing animals are awesome.

The teeth actually developed from scales.

find fossil teeth. What's interesting about those teeth is that they're not like our teeth. They developed from scales that, through the evolutionary process, have migrated into the mouth.

We wanted to tag this shark, right at the base of the dorsal fin. But just as suddenly as it appeared, the great white slid off into the depths and was gone. Sean never had a chance to tag it.

Let's leave the great white behind and move a little closer to shore.

Kelp grows like a forest here.

Sea otters are everywhere near the coast.

Here we're drifting over the canopy of a forest—a kelp forest. The kelp, a seaweed, is anchored by hold-fasts to the rocky ocean bottom along this part of the California coast. We're here to see some wonderful creatures, very intelligent members of the weasel or polecat family. They're southern sea otters, marine mammals that spend much of their lives in the ocean from the coastline to about 3 miles out, in depths of about 200 feet of water or less.

Check out this underwater forest.

Here I am out on the water with the otters.

Sea otters actually know how to use tools.

Here's what's neat about the sea otters: Not only are they good hunters and good foragers, but they also are excellent tool users. They'll go down to the bottom, grab a critter with a tough shell, and bring it up. Then they'll pick up a rock or whatever is at hand, and turn the rock into a tool to crack open that shell and have a nice dinner.

This otter has what appears to be a crab, and he's breaking that crab up with his hand, crunching on that crab. But he also has a little battle going on because he has got a seagull hanging over his shoulder like a bad shadow, waiting to grab his food.

Sea otters need to eat a lot because this water is cold and they use up a lot of calories keeping warm. We think of California as being a warm place, but as they say in Santa Cruz, "Dude, the water's cold, man." Sea otters aren't blubbery. They rely on dense fur, thousands and thousands of individual strands of hair per square inch. And they continually groom that fur, bring the oils around the hair to create a barrier that keeps the warmth in and the cold out.

This guy has a seagull trying to figure out how to steal that crab.

Next we'll head inland, to the mountains that surround Mammoth Lake, to meet another of California's incredible predators....

Sierra Nevada Mts.

Mammoth Lakes

The Sierra Nevada mountains are home to tons of wild animals.

California is a huge state, but nearly 34 million people live here. All these people put huge pressure on the environment. Many of the creatures here are fighting for their lives. The great natural beauty of the Sierra Nevada mountains has turned this part of the state into a booming resort area—and that boom has turned one of California's greatest predators into an unwanted pest.

I love this habitat. We're surrounded by these towering

ponderosa pines. It's quiet. You feel safe—but that sense of safety's deceiving. If you were here with me now, you could smell a musky aroma, the aroma of a black bear...

Scratched up trees are a sure sign you're in bear country.

A bear clubhouse...

And here's further evidence that we are in prime bear country: A bear has been ripping away at this ponderosa, to the point that it's tilting. It's going to fall pretty soon. The bear has been pulling the wood away to get the insect larvae that live and grow inside it. He chomps the wood into pulp, extracts the protein, and he's got quite a nice meal.

Check this out. We have an abandoned house, which has been left to rot and has become a valuable place of residence for a bear.

Here's a big guy, close up.

A bear's been at this couch.

A smart bear has made a den under here.

…There's bear scat. And look at this couch. It's completely disheveled. All the upholstery and stuffing have been pulled away, and I think I know why.

The bear that's using this house has created his den underneath it, right underneath the porch. Talk about a creative, smart-thinking bear. He's pulled all the stuffing from that couch, and he's brought it down to his den and lined his bed. He's also raided the bedroom of this place—so when he goes to bed he rests his bear head on a pillow. It shows you how these animals are just masters at survival.

Here's me and my bear scat.

Here's that juice pack...

Look at this. I've found a big pile of bear scat still warm, still steaming. You can see what this animal's been eating. You can tell that human beings have crossed the path of this bear, because he ate a little juice pack—and I'm telling you, he ate the whole juice pack.

I can hear some clawing, some gnawing sounds. The bear is coming through, and if we're lucky we'll see him.

A beautiful black male...

And there he is—it's a big old boar, a male bear. He's quick to flee and heads up a tree—these great creatures are excellent climbers. That's a beautiful black bear. He probably weighs 350 or 400 pounds. I can hear him huffing and puffing, letting us know that he knows we're here. He is demonstrating what I hope is a bluff—saying "I'm bigger than you. I'm larger than life."

See his lip curl up and quiver? That's called *flemen*. Quivering his lip like that helps him register scents with his extraordinary sense of smell. This creature can detect the presence of bird's eggs in that tree with his nose. And if he finds them, he'll eat them. At this time of year he's stocking up, packing on that body fat, building his energy reserve for the winter.

Right now it looks like this one is taking a nap. A black bear... you can live alongside these animals, enjoy their natural history, and cherish it.

He smells me... even way up there.

Looks like I bored this bear...

Here's my friend Bryan.

Head south and west from the Sierra Nevadas, and just before you fall into the ocean you'll find yourself in Hollywood, a land of sun, fun, starlets, and make-believe. Tourists flock here to see the stars. I'm no different, but I like to mix my star gazing with snake hunting. I'm here with a friend of mine, actor Bryan Cranston, from the television show *Malcolm in the Middle.* He's dressed to hunt snakes Hollywood-style, with a pitching wedge for a snake stick.

We're going to
go look through this
rocky area and see if
we can find us a nice
rattlesnake. This is
good snake habitat,
with lots of crevices
where they can hide.
These snakes can
sense body heat, so if
they're here they're
probably aware of
our presence.

And there's some-
thing in here....

It's a southern
Pacific rattlesnake.
Check it out. That
rattle developed at
the end of the Ice Age,
and it was the snakes'
way to warn buffalo

Here, snake, snake...

Can you see the Pacific
rattlesnake in there?

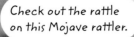

Check out the rattle on this Mojave rattler.

not to step on them. That's the purpose it served for thousands of years, but rattlesnakes today are less likely to rattle. That's because a snake that rattles today identifies itself to a human being, which could kill it. So the rattlesnakes that rattle are killed, and the ones that don't rattle survive and then pass on that trait to the next generation.

The Pacific rattlesnakes are a beautiful greenish color.

These southern Pacific rattlesnakes are also called green rattlesnakes, and if you look at the belly you can see a kind of green tinge. This guy's probably about eight or nine years old, an adult male. He's about 2 $\frac{1}{2}$ to 3 feet long, but these snakes can grow up to 4 or 5 feet in length.

You want to keep at a safe distance from a snake like this. If you were out walking around and saw this snake coiled up, and if you heard a rattle, that would mean he's alarmed and doesn't want you messing with him. He might strike.

We're going to head next to one of Los Angeles' chi-chi suburbs. Somewhere in that neighborhood is a bobcat that thinks he owns the place....

Thousand Oaks is home to lots of wildlife.

Wildlife rangers are picking up a signal...

Thousand Oaks takes great pride in having a lot of open space. They call it the greenbelt, and it provides some great natural habitat for wildlife. Of course, there can be problems when these wild neighbors meet their human counterparts. What's amazing is that city people move to this suburban environment because they want to be close to nature, and when they get close they want to kill the animals.

Seth and Piper are wildlife rangers who monitor the health and safety of the predators that share this high-priced real estate. Piper's picking up signals from a transmitter collar that the rangers placed on one of the bobcats here.

And now we see it—a male bobcat—and until it moved, it looked like a rock. We track it going right along a fence line, into a yard, and onto the sidewalk.

He looks right at me... not frightened at all.

It's a good-sized cat, probably 20 to 25 pounds. Look at that—it stopped and looked right at me for a moment. It wasn't even frightened. This is part of its home range.

I'm as excited as if I discovered a leopard or an African lion. Maybe it wasn't a dangerous encounter, but what was special about this bobcat is that it has adapted, has married its life with the human world as well as the wild world. And that's what this was all about.

Follow the highway east from Los Angeles and you'll end up in the desert—not just any desert, but the Mojave Desert. So far California has offered us some animals that are struggling to coexist with their human neighbors, but out here in the desert we can get away from civilization for awhile.

The desert in bloom...

Mojave Desert

◆ **Palm Springs**

This habitat looks empty, but it's full of life.

The Mojave just looks desolate. In reality it's teeming with life. Just now a Mojave green rattlesnake disappeared under a rock, flattening his body and tucking it under. Mojave rattlesnakes have excellent camouflage, which allows them to blend in with this gravelly land-scape. I'm going to pull him out again.

These guys are serious looking.

I have to be very, very careful, because of all the rattlers this is one of the most venomous. Many of the rattlers have what we call hemotoxic venom, which destroys body tissue. This guy is different.

You have to be super careful with these snakes.

It has a very potent venom, which is part hemotoxic, part neurotoxic. Not only does the venom break down body tissue, but it also slows down the nervous system.

Even the small snakes are toxic.

Even though this one's a small snake, its venom is as toxic as that of an adult. In fact, in some cases smaller snakes can be more toxic than bigger snakes of the same species because as a snake ages the venom degrades, or breaks down. This snake can also control the amount of venom it injects when it bites. Maybe it will inject no venom. Maybe it will inject copious amounts.

Check out the camouflage on this guy.

The biggest indicator that you're dealing with the Mojave rattler and not a western diamondback is the head. A western diamondback, or an eastern diamondback for that matter, has a larger, more triangular head. That's a good thing to note, since the Mojave rattler's venom is so much more potent.

Look at the shape of the head.

There's something else I want to show you. If you ever thought it was tough to move around with legs, then you should look at the way a snake moves. This is a limbless reptile, but it uses powerful muscles that run along its body and are connected with its skin to move in what we call concertina fashion. It gathers and extends just like an accordion.

The Mojave rattlesnake—yes, it's a venomous critter, but it sure is beautiful and a very valuable resident of this important ecosystem, the Mojave Desert.

LOOK AT THIS!

Rattlesnakes and other venomous snakes get a bad rap. Because they are potentially dangerous, most people think these creatures are mean. But they're just like any other snake—trying to survive. They get dangerous when they feel threatened by another animal—whether that animal is an eagle, a mongoose, or a human. As a threat to humans, rattlesnakes are not high on the list. Each year there are about eight hundred reported cases of rattlesnake bites. Of these reported bites, only one to two cases result in death. And the majority of rattlesnake bites are successfully treated with as little as two to three days of hospitalization.

So what can a person do to prevent a snake bite? Hands, feet and ankles are the most common sites for rattlesnake bites. Using some common sense rules can prevent most snakebites:

· Never go barefoot or wear sandals when walking in the rough. Always wear hiking boots.
· Always stay on paths. Avoid tall grass, weeds, and heavy underbrush where there may be snakes.
· Always look for concealed snakes before picking up rocks, sticks, or firewood.
· Always check carefully around stumps or logs before sitting.
· When climbing, always look before putting your hands in a new location. Snakes can climb walls, trees, and rocks and are frequently found at high altitudes.
· Never grab "sticks" or "branches" while swimming. Rattlesnakes are excellent swimmers.
· Baby rattlesnakes are poisonous! They can and do bite. Leave them alone.
· Never tease a snake to see how far it can strike. You can be several feet from the snake and still be within striking distance.
· Learn to respect snakes and to leave snakes alone. Curious children who pick up snakes are frequently bitten.
· Always give snakes the right of way!

This is one of my favorite reptiles.

This reptile is designed to survive in a really tough environment.

Look at this really cool, awesome reptile—one of my favorites. This ancient-looking creature is the desert tortoise. You find this animal living in the southwestern parts of the United States, in the high desert of California all the way down to Arizona and parts of New Mexico. It's perfectly designed to survive in this very tough environment. This animal spends

This guy can go for long periods without drinking.

about 90 to 95 percent of its life under-
ground to escape the dangerously hot desert sun. Because it
can conserve water, it can go for long periods without drinking.

The shell helps the tortoise conserve water. It's divided
into two parts—the carapace, the top part of its shell, and the

Look at this shell.

plastron, the plate underneath. When these creatures turn upside down, they'll flip their heads up and rock their limbs to try to turn themselves right side up.

These guys are solid.

Here's something else that's interesting about these creatures: Their legs are built almost like the columns of a Greek temple, because their bodies are very heavy. They need to support that heavy mass, and they do that with solid, elephant-like (or elephantine) legs and wide feet to distribute the weight.

Strong legs to carry a heavy body.

The desert tortoise—a gorgeous creature. We'll place him back where we found him. He can continue foraging, and we can continue to explore California.

Real estate development has put pressure on wildlife.

We can monitor the bighorn sheep from the air.

Just a nine-iron shot from that rocky desert is the fun-in-the-sun mecca of Palm Springs. The growth of this resort boomtown is putting pressure on another California creature, the peninsular bighorn sheep. Peninsular bighorn sheep are one of the most endangered ungulates in North America. The total population is around four hundred. In this area there's a tiny population of bighorns, only about twenty-five individuals. Scientists are monitoring these animals in hopes of saving them. That means finding them and then, even more difficult, capturing them and bringing them back to biologists at base camp for tagging and testing. It's challenging, dangerous, and exciting stuff.

We're hunting for bighorn with the scientists in a pair of helicopters, a chase helicopter and another for monitoring. These animals are hard to spot on the desert mountain slopes because they blend in. There could be a ram right below us weighing 200 pounds, but against that brown landscape it disappears.

This is the monitoring copter.

The bighorns are tough to spot from the air.

A net gun captures the animal.

Here comes the sheep...

Once the team spots a bighorn, the first chopper moves in and fires a net gun to capture the animal. Then the second chopper comes in to secure the sheep. The terrain is too rough to land, so we have to jump out of the chopper.

The sheep aren't sedated, but a blindfold keeps them from getting too freaked out as they're airlifted to the base camp.

Back at the base camp, veterinarians and researchers gather all the data they need as quickly as they can. They've got to move very, very quickly because these animals are not anesthetized.

We have two animals here—a ram, which is a male, and a ewe, a female, which is smaller and more delicate, with smaller horns.

The guy with the yellow jumper is Jim DeForge of the Bighorn Institute, which has worked to save the peninsular bighorn sheep from extinction since 1981. He has a long swab that he'll insert in the nasal cavity of this sheep to take a mucus sample. The vets will do a culture study of that sample to see if this creature has acquired any respiratory diseases. These animals are vulnerable to disease, and the researchers want to know if any diseases they carry are naturally occurring or introduced by outside agents, such as cattle.

This is Jim.

We'll check this back at the lab.

You can see the radio collar here.

This animal is marked with a tag in its left ear, and it has a collar around its neck that sends out a radio signal, using satellite-based GPS (global positioning system) technology. In this region, even though this creature is a master of survival, it's so close to extinction that there are only eight females left. That's why this study is so important.

Isn't this ram spectacular?

And this beautiful ram is a perfect example of what makes these animals so spectacular. We're just going to let him leave when he's ready, on his own accord.

California has proved to be a great experience. Not only have we witnessed conservation in action, but we also got to be close to one of the rarest animals living in California, the peninsular bighorn sheep. I'll see you again on our next wildlife adventure!

Glossary

anesthetized put to sleep or numbed by a drug

apex the highest point

canopy the top layer of a rain forest or kelp forest

carrion the remains of a dead animal

cartilaginous composed of or related to cartilage

copious a large amount

ecosystem a community of organisms

evolutionary Process how animal species adapt and change over time

extinction when no more members of a species are alive

foragers animals that wander and search for food on the ground

fossils remains of ancient animals found in the earth's crust

GPS Global Positioning System

habitat a place where animals and plants live naturally together

hemotoxic venom that damages blood and tissue

holdfasts the parts a plant uses to attach itself to a surface

kelp forest an underwater habitat made up of kelp

neurotoxic venom that damages the nervous system

predators animals that kill and eat other animals

reptile a cold-blooded, usually egg-laying animal such as a snake or lizard

respiratory related to breathing

scat animal droppings

tallow animal fat

venomous having a gland that produces poison for self-defense or hunting

Index